Mum, we wanted your book of poetry to be shared,
to touch other hearts as you have touched ours.
Our world is a much richer place because of you.

Proverbs 31:29 Many daughters have done virtuously,
but thou excellest them all.

We are blessed, David, Heather, Paula, and Andy.

My Home My England

M.A.F. Ketley

To Jack.
ith All my
Love

4

My Home My England

There's a corner of old England
which to me is always home,
It isn't quaint or beautiful
But I feel its all my own.

I know the little byways
The lanes and hedges all,
The way they are dressed in Springtime
As well as in the fall.

Wild roses in profusion grow
White clover spreads the lane.
While trunks of trees with ivy green
Comes back to mind again.

There's the village school with bricks of red
Where I began at three
to leave my Mother's apron strings
Till it was time for tea.

With lessons done, we used to run,
Behind the Churchyard stones
And spring upon our friends with glee
With ghastly sobbing moans.

Where twin paths met there stood a tree
Beside – a plaque to prove-
'Twas planted by a royal prince
Who later gave up all, for love.

'Twas just a small oak sapling
Though frail and tender then
Has grown so fine and splendid
And outlived scores of men.

Majestic still the grey Church stands
Described by many pens
As "Queen of all the Marshlands"
"Cathedral of the Fens".

I'm looking for a cottage small
Its hearth so warmly glowed
But in its place there stands a house
All signs of "Home" removed.

With eyes a little misty
I stroll down memory lane,
And know as sure as lilacs bloom
I'd choose "This spot" again.

M.A.F. Ketley

A Silent Prayer

Oh God! Who made this earth so fair,
Didst thou foresee the will of man?
Who's only urge to rend and tear
Without the sense to understand,

Whilst ashes of the past still warm
Are fanned into the flame of hate,
No time have they to watch a child
As he stands swinging on the gate.

His blue eyes greet the world each dawn
No fear as yet has touched his heart,
He cannot know the angry storm
Which waits to tear his world apart.

Oh! Give him time to know the joys
The simple things which are his right,
The right with other girls and boys
To walk by day towards the light.

M.A.F. Ketley

To Jackie
(Reassuring Jack of her love during their long seperations)

Oh! Hearken love that you might hear
Straight from my heart and it is true,
A story whispered in your ear
I have no thought of none – but you.

And darling should you doubt my heart,
Then raise your eyes and in them look,
And in their depths read all sweetheart,
For you they are an open book,

Then having read, believe it dear,
And hold it as a memory true,
And maybe when our hearts are near
You'll whisper "Dearest I love you".

M.A.F. Ketley

A Better World

Oh! Mighty waves of war roll on
That in thy ending I may see,
The glory of a better world
For all that I hold dear to me.
A world wherein but peace is known
Of love and joy and tenderness,
To those whose faith is well renowned
Bring nothing ere but happiness.

M.A.F. Ketley

The Great love

Many moons and many years
Will pass again before –
A love like ours will reappear
And then my dear what's more –
Only if this son of ours
We call by name of David,
Should take his heritage from you
And not by time have faded,
But bloom anew when he's a man
The great love you yourself began.

M.A.F Ketley
Written to Dad

Watching and Waiting

From dawn till dusk I lift my eyes
To gaze up far into the skies
For in them rides – beneath the sun
My heart, my life my only one

I've found him there oft times before
In peaceful times before the war
A gay salute with tilted wing
Which made my heart a dancing thing.

Now duty takes him far away
But still I'm hoping that some day,
Once more I'll see with happy eyes
My dearest there in friendlier skies.

But better still I hope far more,
To see him standing at our door,
The dearest face I ever knew
To smile with me my whole life through.

M.A.F Ketley

Written to Dad.
F/Lt J. Ketley
(pilot)

Remember Darling

Each star that shines upon your way,
Each moonbeams' friendly gleam,
Will tell you that I love you still –
Enfolded in a dream.

M.A.F. Ketley

Longing

I need the comfort of thine arms
The nearness of thy dearest charms,
The sweetness of a lover's kiss
Oh yes! My dear I need all this
And more besides were I to tell
The dreams that in my heart do dwell,
Caresses tender, warm and true,
To help me all the long day through,
And with the coming of the night
When birds begin their homeward flight.
I long to hold you to my heart
My dearest – never more to part

M.A.F. Ketley

Dearest Of All

I love thee with my heart, with my arms
With my eyes and with my soul.
I love all I know of thee and all I've yet to learn.
All there has been, and all there is to be.
I need thee as the rainbow needs the sun,
birds the trees, and flowers the gentle rain.
With thee, life could reach a zenith of
Perfect happiness – to be held most dear to
One's heart, and cared for as a treasured possession,
Like a beautiful rose- whose perfume is
Too strong ever to be forgotten.
Yet whose substance is too fragile to
Risk hurting by lack of love and attention.
In all these ways do I love thee? –
And softly from out of nowhere, comes an echo
Sealing all this happiness within my heart – forever.

M.A.F. Ketley

A La Leave

Its leave my Jackie boy once more,
And Oh! What fun we have in store.
We'll play and dance, and shout and sing
In fact we'll do most everything.
At dawn we'll argue who's to be
The first to make the grade for tea,
And after brekker – sweep and dust,
Then do the veg. For that's a must.

And after lunch we'll take a rest,
For that's the time we're not our best.
The thought of washing up my dear
Is not a pleasant one I fear.
But renewed with energy,
We'll tackle it most reverently,
If you'll not come up from the rear
And try to bite lumps from my ear.

Then to the garden we must go,
To have a look around you know,
There isn't much to see right now
But later on – Boy what a wow!
Now its time for tea once again
What shall we have we both complain,
Some radishes No! They're not through
Perhaps some bread and cheese will do!

Where do the children come in this?
I know they're dying for a kiss,
So let's look around and see if we
Can find out just where they can be.
And now its bedtime for them both
Although you know they are quite loath,
To go to bed is not their idea
Of having lots of fun – no fear!

But once we've got them off to bed
And kissed each little sleepy head,
We'll say "Night Night" to both our joys
And "God Bless all our Bomber Boys"
Then with our chairs not far apart,
We'll draw up by the fire sweetheart
To talk and dream of future bliss,
And then maybe you'll steal a kiss.

And now my darling 'ere we sleep.
Let us to our bedroom creep
To snuggle down amongst the clothes
To, Night Night dear; sweet repose.

M.A.F. Ketley

A Dream

I dreamed I stood upon the shore,
Stood looking out across the sea,
The night was like a velvet cloak
As black as far as eye could see.

And silent as an empty tomb
I gazed as from the darkness there –
Arose the unexpected sight
Of flames with red and angry glare.

I watched not knowing what they meant,
Or if some future it foretold,
I only know the flames were red
And down my spine the sweat ran cold.

M.A.F. Ketley

My Heart's Desire

If only I could write like Burns,
Byron, Shelly, or Rupert Brooke.
Perhaps my heart would cease to yearn
And outward could begin to look.

Though Autumn's cloth of gold is set
Beyond my window pane,
The winds are cold and grasses wet
And I withdraw again.

Withdraw into this shell of mine
A love where none can hope to meet,
To hold my hand in friendship fine
Or make my loneliness more sweet.

How can they understand my heart
When they have lost the key,
Have lost the warmth which was a part-
A part of life – and me.

M.A.F. Ketley

Beloved

Weep not dear heart for it is but awhile
Before we meet again, and you shall see his smile,
Oh! Heart of hearts, Oh! King of my desires!
Withhold me not thy love – but let me at your fires.
Betroth my heart to thee, and promise to be true.
For with my life and soul, I give my all to you,

M.A.F. Ketley

A Man and His Land

When the heart of a man is in the heart of his land.
And he feels he is one with the soil.
Every moment is spent in the sweetest content,
And his work is more pleasure than toil.

At the crack of the dawn, as each new day is born,
He will rise and away to the fields,
He has worries 'tis true but he always pulls through,
Only resting to par-take of meals.

He eats hearty and well, has no need of a bell
To tell him when dinner is served.
He can eat like a horse often just the one course
Has no time for soup, fish and hors d'oeuvres.

He has learned by mistake every move he must make,
To ensure bumper harvest and crop,
And though crippled by pain with the wind and the rain.
Presses on – though his body cries "stop!"

With his tractor and plough he will furrow and sow
Keeping check on the weeds and the pests.
And will nurse from the earth every seed at its birth,
Watch it grow, clean and strong at its best.

With an eye that is keen in a face that is lean
He will scan every inch of his land
And will know in his heart he is really a part
Of God's garden – with God's help, he has manned.

M.A.F. Ketley
Dedicated to my brother David 1960.

14

A Sorrow Shared

Did I feel a tear my love –
and was it shed for me?
And was your heart a little sad –
for one you could not see?
I felt it cool upon my cheek-
It stayed a little while,
I knew your heart was with me then –
Though chained by many a mile.

The bitterness all melts away
When shared with one so dear,
And only sweetness in its stead
When once an aching tear.
A gentle hand, a heart's warm glow,
A smile that leads the way,
A tender word, a loving glance
Walks with me – day by day.

And as I walk - I know my love
Your hand is held in mine
As all the cares of yesteryear
Are brought to your heart's shrine.
And gently I would know your smile
And softly I would feel,
The love I know you bear for me
Was real my love – was real.

M.A.F. Ketley

Conscience

Fool! Fools! That women are
Who cannot conscience bear,
They use their tongues to stab their hearts
Then wonder when and where –
Again a song will pass their lips
A song for joy to sing,
There is no song within my heart,
No song – or anything!

M.A.F. Ketley

Almond Blossoms

Your canopy of clouded pink,
Bursts forth some sunny day,
And holds my heart to ransom, I cannot run away.
As there beneath your blossoms fair
Enchanted still I stand, I long to stand forever,
My soul at your command.

My arms outstretched I try to reach
Your tender petals where –
Caressed by singing birds and bees
Such sweetness find they there.
And I would feel your blossoms cool
Upon my cheek to lie,
Like soft sweet lips they hold me
And take my breath away.

The sun moves on and with it I recall
That should I stand here long enough
Your petals they must fall –
Around my feet they'll gather
As sweet a carpet lay,
Unheeded by the passers-by –
Or children as they play.

Then I will go- and with me I will take
Your image fair upon my heart.
As patiently I wait
Another day, another year.
Your gracious charms
And with me take your promise
That you'll return to me.

M.A.F Ketley

Autumn Reflections

It seems to me now summer's gone
And roses lose their lovely bloom,
A break is due to nature's soil
To sleep and rest a little while.
She's seen the best of summer's sun
And tried to please us everyone
with beauty bright and colours gay
To charm our hearts at each new day.

The rain-kissed rambler passing by,
To chrysies tall is heard to sigh,
"Farewell dear ones my day is gone
what joy is yours now just begun,
While other plants prepare to rest
You wake again with glory dressed.
In colours bright of every hue
Your perfume fresh with morning dew"

But soon when frosts and heavy rain
Have come to stay with us again,
And winter sky is dark with snow
Then even they will have to go.
Nor shall we blame the earth's bare breast
For she has surely earned her rest.
And so we wait till cuckoos sing
To herald in the new born spring.

M.A.F. Ketley

Vision of Delight

See! Two white swans – how beautiful they are.
Majestically they glide – they've come so far,
Their graceful breasts, the curling waters meet.
At the cool streams edge by the meadow sweet.

M.A.F. Ketley

Bejewelled Garden

Through my window with delight
I see them dancing in the light,
Swaying with the morning breeze
Changing colour with brilliant ease.

No crown did sport such beauty fair
Aladdin's cave held naught so rare,
Trembling they hang 'twixt leaf and flower
Making for fairies a heavenly bower.

A sun-drenched haven - where, as they play
Their beauty takes one's breath away.
Ruby, emerald and sapphire,
They gleam and shimmer like liquid fire.

And though I know they cannot stay
Return they will another day,
When morning sun climbs o'er my wall
To kiss the dew drops ere they fall.

M.A.F. Ketley

Unhappy Wanderer

There once lived a hermit all by himself,
He cared not for treasures – of art or wealth
His pillow the bracken, the sky his dome,
Stars light his evenings, Thoughts wander home.

Did they remember his kith and kin,
Remember the fun they had had with him?
Young altogether foolish and glad,
Oh! How his memories made him sad.

Why had he left them to roam on his own?
To lie here in solitude – heart cold as stone.
No love to comfort, no hand to clasp,
Understanding the need – for friendship at last.

M.A.F. Ketley

The Silver Birch

The fairest tree in all the world
Is the silver birch with leaf unfurled,
All winter long like the sheerest lace
Her silvery hair brushed the skies grey face.

Now with the balmy spring-like air
Wears leafy ribbons in her hair,
Green and dainty fluttering high
A garland for the changing sky.

She sighs - the wind sweeps through her boughs,
He is her lover – and she knows
Today though his caress be sweet
Tomorrow he may roughly greet.

So strong his love she hardly hears
The sweetest words poured in her ears,
She trembles through each leaf and branch
And bears his passion in a trance.

M.A.F. Ketley

To Peggy and Al

In a local shop we wandered to make a festive call
When suddenly there twinkled –
These bellows on the wall,
We paused to take a closer look,
We'll swear we heard them say
"Please take us home to Peg and Al –
they need us every day."

In winter when its cold and dull
We'll make their fires glow.
In summer when the skies are bright
We'll hang up just for show.
So Peggy dear and Alan too,
We leave them in your care,
And hope they'll bring much pleasure
For now and many a year.

Dear friends of Audrey and Jack

19

To Tibby

Tibby my darling couldn't you wait for the coming of Spring-
This year so late?
Were you so eager to be on your way
That you couldn't stay with us – just one more day?
Its here Tib! The warmth you waited long for,
The sun's in the corner here by the back door.
The garden you loved soft and fresh with the rain
Will never more be your playground again.
We have loved you so well – the family and I,
And though we all knew you would soon have to die,
We shall miss you so much Tib – no longer old Dear
to see you on window ledge or curled in a chair.
So faithful, forgiving, in spite of our teasing,
Or putting you out – when you carried on sneezing.
You were everything gentle – so pretty and sweet,
from the tips of your ears to your black and white feet.
Goodbye little friend – sweet dreams be all yours.
As you rest with your head on your tiny front paws.
We'll remember you often, with each passing day.
"Evergreen" in our hearts - will our love for you stay.

M.A.F Ketley

3 yr old Heather found a black and white kitten with paint smudges all over her.
Heather brought her home where she was loved for 15 years.

Clair De Lune

There's a boat on the river my loved one!
Coming with me to find,
Where the moon kisses the water,
Leaving the crowd behind.

So still, so sweet is the silence
As together we sail through the night,
Only a breeze whispers softly
As two hearts so fondly unite.

Take my hand then and gently lead me
Through the moonbeam's soft caress,
And there – where the golden light shimmers
Love me – with tenderness.

M.A.F Ketley

Fickle Eve

Women are a fickle lot
But none more so than men,
And none goes in the melting pot
Comes out the same again.

They sweet talk till the cows come home,
Like drops of honeyed dew,
They fool nobody but themselves
To all their "bill and coo".

Some will swear away estates
While others just their hearts,
And in the twinkling of an eye
Forget – once well apart.

And long before the moon is old
They'll do it all again,
Oh! What a fickle lot is "Eve"
But none more so than men.

M.A.F. Ketley

Fairest of All

Oh! Lovely rose – haste not away too soon,
For I would have you grace the path
Of my true love at noon.
She walks to meet me in this bower,
The sunlight in her hair
And sunbeams dancing in her eyes.
She is most wondrous fair
Hark! Hear ye not her gentle step?
See not her form in view?
So slender, sweet, and beautiful,
Far lovelier than you!

M.A.F. Ketley

Heart Of My Heart

Come not to me too vividly,
The sweetness takes my heart away,
And she who lives without a heart
Must live in other worlds apart.

But just to see you there awhile,
To gaze once more at your dear smile,
Is worth a kingdom with a crown
Or banishment to worlds unknown.

M.A.F. Ketley

Eight By Ten

I only have to lift my eyes,
to see a vision sweet,
Of motherhood, her little ones,
so clean so trim and neat.
Her pretty face alight with joy
Her hair like burnished gold,
her eyes so proud as if to say
"These are my life, my world".
There's Markie quite the little man-
Beside his mum so straight.
Sweet Angie holding mummy's hand,
She's holding it so tight.
So much the image of his dad
Dear Mark, his age just three,
Has mummy's arm around his waist
She cares for both so lovingly.
Small Angie born in USA
Has yet to step on English soil,
We're longing for that day.
The day when we can hold them close
Dear mummy, daddy, all.
We'll celebrate in such a way –
We'll really have a ball.
Yet rarely do we think of them
As being far away.
Because our thoughts are full of them
Throughout each night and day,
So thank you God for this small gift
From Thy great bounteous Store,
To have, to hold, to see each day,
To love them all, for evermore.

(Mum 1964)

Erskine Vs Cooper

There they scream and yell for blood
Ten thousand men or more,
The champion slips and finds too soon
He's sprawling on the floor.
Its not what they expected
He quickly tries to rise
And smartly his opponent's glove
Lands yet one more surprise.

His chin meets leather strong and true
He hits the deck again,
The bell has gone – too late they stop-
Joe's manager complains.
Young Cooper stands good six feet tall
He's boxing splendidly
His eyes are cut – but in he goes
And Joe's bashed savagely.

The champ recovers once or twice
Through mists that cloud his brain
And tries to "whip" his lagging heart
Into the fray again.
Though courage he shows throughout
His cause is lost, its felt
He's down! He's out across the ropes
And Cooper wins the belt

M.A.F. Ketley

Deride Me

Deride me – call me names –
Insult me if you will
Through anger my heart flames
I can but love you still.

M.A.F. Ketley

Falling Petals

The city streams with life below
Each neon light is lit,
There – joy and sorrow side by side
is very closely knit.
Some have had a busy day
Others seeking pleasure,
Some have lost the one they love
Or something which they treasure.

Each one has a heart that beats
For someone rather special,
Here, rogue, or vagabond, however superficial
Were this not so- then Heaven knows,
There'd be no point in living
To have, to hold, to share
to feel the joy in giving.

A silhouette against the moon
Stands looking down awhile,
He is alone, and full of care,
And yet I see him smile.
He has a duty to perform
He says a little prayer
Then, from the flower of his heart
Lets fall the petals there.

His thoughts go out to one he loves
He calls her to his side,
She takes his hand and tries to share
The pain he cannot hide.
He knows that other blossoms
Will come to fill his heart,
And so with quiet footsteps
He turns – and then departs.

M.A. F. Ketley

And You Shall Know

Feel the touch of the sun on a winter's day,
See the first Spring buds in the month of May,
Know the joy of a bird as it soars on wing,
And you shall know how my heart doth sing.

Feel the call of the hills as you wend your way
Through the brackened slopes on a fine crisp day,
See the young trout leap as he skims the stream
And you will know how my heart doth dream.

Feel the peace in your heart as you kneel to pray,
Count a million stars in the Milky Way.
Feel the love in my heart so tenderly,
And you shall know what you mean to me.

M. A. F. Ketley

Apparition

I saw you standing there –
And all my heart and soul
Leapt in my eyes,
I saw you standing there
'Twas only vapoured air –
In your disguise.

M. A. F. Ketley

For Thee

Could I but still the hands of time
And stay their fleeting hour,
Or hold the heaven's sun in space,
Could wave aside a shower.

All these I'd do for thee and more
To see a smile upon thy face,
And lay sweet pleasures at thy door
To know the warmth of thine embrace.

I'd search for blossoms rare my love
And spread thy path with fragrance sweet,
And I would pluck the stars for thee
To lay them shimmering at thy feet.

And kings for all their lordly airs
Could be no richer than myself.
Far richer still my heart would be
Than "Midas" with his golden wealth.

For dearly I would see my love
Awakening there within thine eyes,
A world of beauty yet unknown-
The sweetness of love's paradise.

M.A.F. Ketley

(Untitled)

I know the countless tears that fall,
How bitter is the taste of gall.
I too have sipped their saltiness
And know the thorn of loneliness.

M.A.F. Ketley

Heart Break

My heart has cried a million tears
They cease not day or night,
I fain would try to hide the pain
Which struggles to the light.
Sometimes they show in just a sigh
Or in a thoughtless deed.
They sear into my very soul
And burn like fire to reed.

Fanned daily by the winds of fate,
They leave my scorched heart bare,
Relentless in its blazing path
My dreams lie shattered there.
There is no balm could ease the pain
No potion sharp or sweet
Could quench the anger of the flames
Through which my heart doth sweep.

If you must weep – then weep my heart,
And let your rivers flow –
And rise – to fill this aching void -
Which daily seems to grow.

M.A.F. Ketley

Nectar

Did any bee such honey find
As this imparted to my lips,
To taste its sweetness all sublime
I lift my heart for one more sip.

M.A.F. Ketley

28

Hell Hath No Fury!

No longer does the thought of you
Beguile my foolish heart.
The scales have fallen from my eyes
And you no longer stand apart.
I'd pass you in a busy street
And let you travel on your way,
Nor would I give a backward glance
As I would have - just yesterday.

You fooled me for a little while
Believing all those age-old lies,
But now at last, I understand
More thankful than you realize.
So you go your way, and play your game
And have your fun whilst you've the chance,
There'll come a time when you will long
To know the thrill of true romance.

But you will find that you have no claim
To honesty, or faithfulness,
Without these virtues you will find
Your path is strewn with hopelessness.
For whilst 'tis said "all love is blind"
'Tis not so blind it cannot see –
The weakness in a craven's heart
The lack of true sincerity.

M.A.F. Ketley

(Untitled)

If thou thinkest less of me
Than I deserve,
Then take with thee thy heart
And all its mockery
Leave not thy lies – nor yet
Thine image fair,
I'll keep my heart my own-
For none to share.

M.A.F. Ketley

Inconstant Heart

One day it sings so blythe and gay
Its spirit soaring high,
To fly on gold and azure wings
With song birds in the sky.
It finds no task too great for it
All efforts made to win.
The very world is at one's feet,
Sweet heavens portals – beckoning.

Then skies are grey – no reason do they give
For drowning all one's happiness
And eager wish to live,
One's very bones are steeped in pain
Of care and misery,
Am I the one who yesterday –
Could smile so readily?

Fain would I try to understand
The sweetness and the sorrow,
Which one day makes my heart to sing –
Yet fill with tears tomorrow.

M.A.F. Ketley

Let Me Remember

The memory of a summer's day
When the haze is on the rye,
A blue lagoon, or a moonlit bay
When the tide is running high.

A gusty wind as it bends the trees
And the rain as it washes the sky,
And I will be thankful for evermore
For 'twas shared by you and I.

M.A.F. Ketley

Life's Game

You cannot hope to win, my son,
Unless you play the game,
Unless you know the right from wrong
And wear it like a flame.

It isn't always easy, it wasn't meant to be.
But with the will to do your best
You'll do it cheerfully.

There's heaps and heaps of little things
That you can find to do,
To try to ease another's load
Less fortunate than you.

We haven't such a lot of time
Life's span is all too short.
But we can learn to play it well
As in a game of sport.

M.A.F. Ketley

My Heart's a Butterfly

Darling, could I love you more,
I'd know not where to start,
For truth to tell I have no room
For more here in my heart.

I dream of you from morn till night
Sweet thoughts of you alone,
Which makes my heart a butterfly
On wings so high to roam.

Were you to love me less
I could no longer live,
My heart would die, on broken wings
If you'd no love to give.

M.A.F. Ketley

Love Sincere

How dear is this thy love – which holds
My heart today.
Its very sweetness fills my soul
I long for it to stay.
I hold it precious more than crowns
Containing gems so rare.
It brings a peace so blessed-
A peace I long to share.

Take me to your heart again
And never let me know
The tears of anguish I would feel,
If I ever let you go.
Hold me closely to your breast,
Until we breathe as one,
And tell me that you love me -
I need it as the sun.

This loveliness which blooms anew
Within my heart doth flower,
And blossoms into paradise
With every golden hour.
It feels the glow of sweet caress
As only you can give,
And spreads its fragrance in my heart
As long as I may live.

Sweet thoughts take wing
And find him is my plea.
Tell him that I love him –
In all sincerity.
May he feel my presence each and every day.
Knowing that he holds my heart,
Although so far away...

M.A.F. Ketley

My Easter Prayer

Teach me to be patient
Not only with others –
But also with myself,
Teach me to accept the truth
And not to search for something
Believed hidden –
Which is not really there.
Teach me to take a promise
For what it is worth
And not to think the world
Has come to an end – when one is broken.
Teach me to have the courage
To see myself as others see me,
To take a chance – knowing
It may never come off.
And to help others when the
Opportunity arises –
And not to waste time weeping
For its return once it has gone.
Teach me to have faith in others
When doubting myself,
And to accept each moment of peace
As a blessing.
Give me the wisdom to know
When I am at fault,
And the grace not to expect more from life
Than what I am prepared to put into it.

M.A.F. Ketley

Memories

Sweet is the thought of Christmas time,
With all its friendly cheer,
Bringing close the ones we love
The ones we hold most dear.
Mistletoe and holly bough to hang
Upon the walls
Lanterns, laughter, Christmas trees
And firelight recalls –
The memories sweet across the years
When we were young and gay,
The joys and happiness we knew
And shared – that yesterday.

They tell me I'm a dreamer
That life is far too real
To take a peek into the past
And once again reveal –
The gladness that was born to you
when all the world was gay
When moon and stars shone in your eyes
That lovely yesterday
But dream I shall my whole life through
And keep them lovingly
And ever will I greet the dawn
To forge a memory.

And when there's time to sit and dream
While they gaze into space,
With nothing to be glad about
Or see a dear one's face,
I'll weave a spell around the past
And bring it close to me
To hold the golden treasures fast
For all my heart to see.

And you'll be there my darling
To sweeten life's short days,
To bring a glow of happiness
When moonbeams softly play,
And deeper in my heart you'll stay

Forever part of me,
To dream, to hold, to love again –
My Dearest Memory!

M.A.F. Ketley

Morning Glory

The Master Painter in the night
Strode over fields ere it was light,
And with his mystic brush did weave
A wondrous canvas to perceive.

As yet the virgin snow lies deep
No footprint mars its beauty sweet,
As like a bride adorned and gay
Awaits her groom this lovely day.

Pure crystal stems, and branches fair
Which only yesterday were bare,
Now clothed in robes of hoary frost
Each jewell – perfection without cost.

The early sun with rosy hues
Tints hedge and tree tops he goes,
Sparkling gay in morning dress
He journeys onwards to the west.

I can but stare- no words could ere describe-
This lovely scene which darkness tried to hide-
Until the dawn should break with golden light
And Heaven declares this earthly, heavenly, sight.

M.A.F. Ketley

Mother

Dear Mother with your heart of gold
I recall dear memories when of old
Upon your knee you sang to me
A dear old hymn or melody.

I've missed you since I first left home,
To start life's journeies all alone,
I'll never fail your trust in me.
My love will linger till I die.

I thank you dear with all my heart
That's all I can do to impart,
All my stored up love for you,
I know you also love me too.

So may God Bless you Mother dear,
That I may keep you ever near,
To love and guide me once again
Dear Mother, Love was not in vain.

M.A. F. Ketley

My Own Dear Love

I long to dream of you – to hold your hands,
To seek your lips and taste their nectar sweet
To feel the glow your heart in mine commands
Caress your face, or nestle at your feet.

To lift my eyes and find within your own
A message sweet reflected back to mine,
To hear your voice – a dear remembered tone
Repeat "My own dear hearts" in accents kind.

There never was a time – that I recall
When thoughts of you – did not begin my day,
And when the closing hours of evening fall
Your name upon my lips doth fondly play.

M.A.F. Ketley

Mouse Under the Bath

Poor little mouse, it had to be.
You lived in my house and you were free.
I told you, you would have to go,
But did you listen? Oh dear no!

You prowled around and stripped quite bare
My boxed in bath to line your lair
With roses sweet and lilacs blue,
Without a thought that you might rue.

The day you climbed the stairs to make
Your cosy nest, and morsels take.
You should know better mousie dear,
For we cannot abide you here.

You heeded not, now I must steel
My heart, lest I should pity feel,
For you have dined too well my friend.
Goodbye, I feel this is the end.

M.A.F. Ketley

(Untitled)

Pink blossoms like the softest clouds,
Invite the early bee,
And in the gold forsythia
The birds sing merrily

M.A.F. Ketley

Audrey - 3 Years Old   Young Audrey

On Honeymoon

Audrey's mum Mary Jane Harrod

Nanna's 90th birthday

Audrey's 90th Birthday

The day Audrey and Jack became engaged - 1938

Audrey and Jack, with Paula, Heather and Adrew - 1960

Audrey writing to Heather in the U.S.A - 1963

41

My Little friends

I sit and watch the sparrows in my holly tree,
They hop from bough to bough – it seems to me.
Though cold, so cold the wintry wind doth blow.
They take no heed of berries – shining red against the snow.
'Tis true I've scattered crumbs both near and far,
But even so the birds outnumber scraps of bread,
And one would think the berries gone by now
To supplement, or vary it instead.
They sing quite sweetly for my listening ear,
And peep within my window - warm and snug.
I sit and write – and listen to their song,
And Blackie at my feet lies on the rug.
She stays indoors as much as I will allow,
And sleeps before the fire's fierce ruddy glow,
Or speaks to me with great expressive eyes
Aware I understand – and tells me so.
While Tufty lifts her paws and gently treads
Afraid of this white world, yet daring all.
She walks beyond the garden gate awhile.
Returns when threatening skies release fresh fall.
To them this is their home, and I am theirs.
Though each a stray not knowing where they came.
And like the sparrows in the holly tree.
Made me their keeper – the need of me the same.

M. A. F. Ketley

My Pledge

To you my dear I will be true
Come shadow pain or sorrow,
To love you all my whole life through
Each day and each tomorrow.

Though others please my vanity
And seek to hold my heart,
They only touch the least in me
And like the night depart.

No heartache do they leave behind
No sense of loss or pain,
Like passing ships they travel on
Never seen again.

And all the time the ripples fade
Their circles made more distant,
Unlike the sweet love that you gave
Which makes my heart more constant.

Though we may never meet again,
Our ways forever severed,
I'll know your spirit doth remain
By love to mine own tethered

M.A.F. Ketley

Our English Rose

Her smile is like a summer's day
Warm and sweet and sometimes shy,
Her eyes like blue forget –me-nots
Reflecting sunshine from the sky.

And as the summer has her moods
So she has days when storms must brew,
And breathlessly we wait until
Once more the sun comes shining through.

Gracefully – as swallows dive
She walks with beauty as her right.
The Heavens smile for her alone
And roses bloom for her delight.

With happiness we share her love
For him whom God has joined as one,
And blessings rich with boundless joy
They share with us their lovely son.

M.A.F. Ketley

Night

Night is – as night always was,
Dark and full of shadows,
Owls awaken from their sleep
To swoop o'er farm and meadow.

Then hasten all you creatures small,
And to your homes take shelter,
Lest the dark wings in the night
Should cause your feet to falter.

In your holes and burrows deep
Sleep sound, till morning wakens,
Keep within your hollows warm,
For those who stray are taken.

Now he's circling over head
So silently he watches.
One foul swoop – and there he goes
Triumphantly he clutches.

Ranny, rabbit, Leveret, stoat,
Take heed of this my warning,
Or somewhere in your little world
There'll be one less by morning.

M.A.F. Ketley

Oakham Town, Rutland

The glistening streets beneath the bright lamps glow,
The curled up leaves around the corners blow,
The church clock chimes, the hour is half past five,
The wind blows cool, yet only slightly so.
I walk around the shops, still lit for show,
A café bright shines just across the street,
And in I step, for a coffee hot and sweet,
'Tis Saturday, and as the folks stroll by,
To queue for cinema, or local dances try.
The market place is swept to make it clean,
And make it fit for Sunday all serene.
I spend an hour or so just walking round,
And in a corner of the market place I found
A ring of cobblestones shine damply there.
And one could feel the atmosphere
Of peasants from a far-off market day
Who brought their daily produce to display,
Butter firm and nut brown eggs and cheese,
With fresh sweet milk, in shining pans to please.
There too a grim reminder of the law,
When stocks were used to help to curb the poor.
My fingers touched the curves made smooth by use.
Imagining, the curses and abuse.
A sadness crept throughout my chilling bones,
I felt 'twas time I left behind the glistening stones.
And sought the company of a local inn,
Where I had planned to meet my eldest son.
"The Wheat Sheaf" is a place where one may sit.
And talk or watch the firelight flit
Upon the many brasses on the wall.
A friendly place is Oakham town.
So little time, had I to look around,
But what I saw, just whets my appetite
To learn of more, than can be found in one short night.

M.A.F. Ketley

Our Heritage

I see the flame of copper beech
Her tallest boughs beyond the reach
Of mortals such as you and I
Except to reach it with an eye.

The grand old oak who through the years,
Has seen so many worldly cares,
A hundred decades he has known
And still a hundred more to come.

And chestnuts blazing in our parks
Have candles glowing rich with sparks
Of candy pink or creamy white
A feast for any lordly sight.

The weeping willow leans down low
Embracing gently pools below
Her tears are dried by summer suns
While moorhens shelter in her fronds.

How dreamy would the skyline be
Without the beauty of a tree
Especially in our low-land Fens
No architect could make amends.

The limes that line our avenues
The constant watch of churchyard yews,
All these and many more I see
Great treasures here for you and me.

We take our trees so much for granted
These sentinels which time has planted
To add sweet pleasure to our days
And lift our hearts in love and praise.

M.A.F. Ketley

Parted

How shall I tell thee all my heart
When miles of land or sea must part,
Canst lend thine ear to breezes sweet
My message – dearest love to greet?

Or list. To birds upon the wing
Tell softly how my heart doth sing
For knowing thee hath brought such joy
Ten volumes could not magnify.

Shouldst thou my heart needst tell thy love
A myriad stars await thy mood,
And when the moon is pale on high
Bid her to stay – Believe 'tis I.

And let the rustle of the leaves,
That tremble down to touch thy sleeves
In Autumn, kiss thee as they pass,
'Tis their delight – not mine alas.

But thou shalt know as days go by
My love is with thee constantly,
In heart, in head and hand in hand-
All this my dear – Please understand.

M.A.F. Ketley

(Untitled)

Pink clusters of cherry and almond
As sweet as the blush of a rose,
Transform all the streets
And the gardens so neat
And away with the daffies that blows.

M.A.F. Ketley.

Paula

She's as sweet as an April morning
When the sun shines after rain,
As gay as a daffa-down-dilly
That dances to March – wind's refrain.

She's as fair as the corn in the summer
The hair on her shoulders lies long,
Plaited and tied with red ribbon
Tossed in the air like a song.

As slim as the willows in Springtime,
She leans as she's poised on her toes.
Today she's a great ballerina
Tomorrow? Well nobody knows!

She's kind and she laughs like a bubble
That bursts when it rises too high,
Loves rain – all four legged creatures
Runs errands without asking "why"?

One day she will find like the others
She has wings that she's eager to try,
And away she will go to discover
All those castles she's built in the sky.

Perhaps she'll be a fine dancer,
Paint pictures – A writer of books,
Or maybe she'll just be a dreamer
Content to count stars in the brooks.

Whatever she does I am certain
She'll find friends wherever she goes,
Making their lives all the sweeter
As the sun, as it blesses the rose.

M.A.F. Ketley
(youngest daughter)

Primroses

I saw a sign of spring today,
Although its still November.
'Twas peeping through the rich brown soil
Beneath a leaf of amber.
Just three small spears of green so young
Its dainty flowers concealed.
Beneath the earth's sweet breast my love
Until by spring revealed.
Its sweet and tender blossoms there –
Are waiting for the sun
To match its splendour in the sky
By "starlets" of its own.
It nestles quietly where it lies
My heart awaits its coming
I know the joy my eyes will see
When cuckoos start their roaming.
The countryside will be aglow
Down banks and 'neath green hedges,
Their yellow petals like the sun
By roadside and low edges.
'Tis good to feel the hope again
That rises with the spring
To know the happiness I store –
When blackbirds start to sing.

M.A.F. Ketley

Promise of Spring

Sweet aconites and snowdrops white
Beneath the waking trees,
Brings gladness to our waiting hearts
For heralds of Spring are these.
Then all the world will sing with joy
The birds burst into song,
And leafy trees and flowering shrub
Will sigh "we've slept too long".

White-blossomed pear, and apple sweet
Touched with a rosy glow,
Will spread the tidings far and wide
And everyone shall know –
That once again the world is new
We've yet another chance,
To gather all this loveliness
For sweet remembrances.

To hold it to our hearts awhile
To breathe the fragrant air,
And feel the petals as they fall.
As soft as Angel's hair.
And buttercups like golden stars
Will call the passing bees
And with the daisies sweet and shy
Will lure them from the trees.

Grey skies will turn to hazy blue
With fluffy clouds on high,
While larks will hover in their flight
And trill for you and I.
The sun will kiss the red, red rose
Bejewelled with morning dew,
And deep within the heart of it
I'll find the heart of you.

M.A.F. Ketley

Proud Heart

There comes a time in all our lives
When sorrow plays a part,
A broken toy, a dear one lost,
Not least a broken heart.
Its part of life's kaleidoscope
The dim stars with the bold,
That weaves a richness quite unknown
With beauty yet untold.

We run to cry at mother's knee
When small things go awry,
And later shed with heavy heart
Our tears for him to die
We fall in love and feel for sure
This time its all supreme,
But overnight we sadly learn
'Twas nothing but a dream,

We hide the ache the best we can
As time goes fleeting past
But though we show the world a smile
The pattern's weaving fast.
The rosy reds were happy times
The blues were quieter days,
The gold was when your baby smiled
And shed the sunniest rays.

The grey was when you lost your love
And knew the darkest cloud,
But still – you held your head up high
Humbled, yes – but proud.

M. A. F Ketley

Redbreast

A lovely little robin came to visit me today,
He hopped around the corner
And chirped as if to say,
"Good morning pretty lady
how nice to see your smile.
I rather like your garden
I think I'll stay awhile."

I said "I'd be delighted"
He cocked his cheeky head
And then began to search around
For tiny scraps of bread.
He hopped upon a flower pot
And trilled with all his might.
He made himself at home – at once
He made a charming sight.

My tom cat eyed him cunningly
He knows a thing or two,
But robin showed he could be wise
And up and up he flew.
He settled on the garden shed
Perched high from pussy's claws-
He winked one beady little eye-
And Pom Pom – strolled in doors.

M.A.F. Ketley

Springtime

Small lambs mid the grass and the daisies
In meadows all sprinkled with dew,
Skip high till their tails nearly brush the sky
And somehow the whole world seems new.

M.A.F. Ketley

River Nene

Swiftly flowing, muddy river
Murky skies reflected there,
Screaming seagulls skimming o'er you
Old men, dreaming, stand and stare.

Swirling through the town, you wander,
Never silent, never still,
Seeking, searching, never finding,
Reeds to hamper by the mill.

Black-billed swans adore your waters
As you near the countryside,
Snowy-breasted as the Artic
Gracefully they meet the tide.

On you travel ever-winding
Through the fenlands wintry scenes,
Raindrops falling, sadly falling –
Down this way they brought a Queen.

Brought her to a fine Cathedral,
There to lay her down to rest,
Caring not they had behead her,
Spilling blood upon her breast.

Did you add your salty tears
To those she may have shed that day,
By the Castle where you wandered
Through the fields of Fotheringay.

M.A.F. Ketley

Rogue Cat

He comes to pay his daily call
His eyes are all aglare
He's really very frightened
But now controls his fear.
I grieve to see him on the prowl
Uncertain where to find
The scraps of food he needs so much
Which others leave behind.

His coat is black and very thin
His ears are bitten too.
He jumps at every little thing
And roams the whole day through.
He has no home to call his own
No name to call him by,
But when he stops to look at me
He meets a friendly eye.

Today for just a little while
He sat upon my step
And lost his worried, frightened look
Like any other pet.
I gave him milk and left him there
To drink it at his will,
He lapped it up and slunk away
To lick a greasy gill.

The children always welcome him
They wish that he would stay,
Defensive, wary, and alert
He only slinks away.
Perhaps one day he'll come to know
We would not do him harm.
And rest beneath our windowsill
Where morning sun lies warm.

M.A.F Ketley

Santa's Cold

Old Santa has a heavy cold his nose is like a cherry
His eyes are running like a stream,
He's feeling far from merry.
But like the gentleman he is, he pulls himself together
And with his reindeers willing help
Sets out to face the weather.

He cracks his whip and yells "yo – ho!
Make way we're late in starting",
Just see the swirling snow flakes fly.
They start his cheeks a-smarting.
But though he's cold - so very cold
His heart is warmly glowing,
He swings his sleigh across the skies
Quite sure of where he's going.

He sees a building big and square-
Inside are children sleeping
Except the ones who lie in wait
Through half closed eyes a-peeping.
They watch as from his sack so full
He spills the toys – so many
They wonder in their little hearts
If he is left with any

For all those other girls and boys
Who still await his coming.
But Santa has a ready store and works till early dawning.
How his old face would light with joy
If he could stay to see
The wonder in those kiddies' eyes
As they gaze gleefully-
At all the good things he has left
To fill their happy days.
They love old Santa – to a child
With simple homage – sing his praise.

M.A.F. Ketley

Running Stream

The mind is like a babbling brook
That washes o'er the pebbles,
Cooling clean, and cooling clear
Whilst on and on it travels.

Hindered by the weeds of stress
And held back by the rushes
Still it laughs and makes its way
Kissed warm as south wind passes.

The sunshine of a heavenly day
Makes still the shadows deeper
And sheltered in the heart of time
Are memories all the sweeter.

M.A.F. Ketley

September

Oh! Sweet and lovely Autumn
With your showers of golden rain,
Winging high to kiss the sky
Then whirling down again.

Dappled sun and shadows long
Lay silent in the parks,
While children leave their swings to catch
The flying amber sparks.

They nestle on the pavements
So thickly lying there,
A deep fine russet carpet
Both prince and beggar share.

Spiked ripening conkers one by one
Fall heavy to the ground.
To break the morning silence,
Just waiting to be found.

Their rich brown glossy newness,
Beside an outworn husk,
Are pounced upon with whoops of joy
From dawn to early dusk.

Once more the scent of burning brush
Of rosewood and the thorn
Assail my long forgotten dreams
Of days now past and gone.

When I as just a little child
Ran wildly through the leaves
With eager shuffling footsteps
Beneath the naked trees.

The sun whose days are growing short
Still lingers lovingly,
Caressing every leaf and blade,
With warmth so tenderly.

I've known the seasons one by one,
With gifts, each one has blessed,
Of all the seasons that I love –
I love the Autumn best.

M.A.F. Ketley

To David Heather Paula and Andrew

I wouldn't be your age again
For all the tea in China.
To have four children just like you
Is infinitely finer.

Ha! Ha!
Mum.

Snow Blossoms

'Tis sweet to know you love me dear,
And through the passing day,
hold you warmly to my breast
To dream the hours away.

Remembering every little word
And every little look,
As dearly needed by my heart
As water to the brook.

In dreams I 'll keep our rendezvous
And seek to hold you close,
Willing you to stay with me
As dew stays with a rose.

Until the sun himself awakes
To call and say "Hello !"
And make my dreams reality
Like blossoms in the snow.

M.A.F. Ketley

Spring

When you wake up on an English morning,
And you gaze at an English sky,
And the birds on the wing,
Bring a message of Spring,
And the breeze is as soft as a sigh.
You will notice the greening of hedgerows
And the sparrows a-twittering there,
And the leadening sky
Like a canopy high –
Makes each bud stand out bold and clear.
Each one has a promise of beauty,
Each blossom a joy to behold,
And the girlies naïve
Wear their hearts on their sleeve –
And the boys do the same I am told.

M.A.F. Ketley

Summer Fantasy

It would be so sweet my love to lie
With you and hear the grasses sigh,
And watch the "Painted Lady" fly
As she glides softly by.
And hear the bees a- humming
As they busily seek,
The golden dusted blossoms
Their honey sweet to make.

They have no thought of yesterday
Or cares for the tomorrow,
They live their lives in one bright day
And flit from flower to flower.
The sun shines with a golden haze
Upon their gilded wings,
And further in a woodland glade
A mating cuckoo sings.

Go not dear love, stay yet awhile
And see! How moon and stars do smile.
Upon us as we lie content
With happy hours behind well spent.
I feel your head upon my breast
Sweet breezes fill the air,
And I would love you till I die
With richness full – and fair.

If I were just a honey bee
And had one day to live,
I'd take the sweetness from the flowers
As much as they could give.
And in the summer's shinning rays
I'd make my honey sweet.
And give it all to you my love
In your dear heart to keep.

And when the summer comes again
List!, hear the blossoms say,
Remember her! Remember her!
Who loved you yesterday.

M.A.F. Ketley

Summer Love

Hold fast my love to those few precious hours,
Remember them and like a fragrant flower
Refresh them now and then –
With one sweet - bitter tear,
Not with regret,
But with a love we share.

They shall not die within this heart of mine,
But day by day will soften all I do,
And gently like a cup of warming wine
Will ease my pain –
And make my heart to glow.

There are no words could tell you how I care,
No legioned love –
Could with my love compare,
For what it's worth my heart is yours alone
Take it – lest if with me it stay –
It turns to stone.

M.A.F. Ketley

Sunshine and Shadows

In castles high above the sky,
I dwell awhile within,
And saw the gleaming turrets
No shadows made them dim.

The nightingales sang sweetly
In trees of evergreen.
The flowers bloomed in gardens rare
In the land of might have been.

The fleecy clouds were soft and white,
Tipped here and there with gold,
They played above the castles tall,
The sun had made them bold.

But then the winds changed suddenly
The fleecy clouds were gone.

The nightingales sang out no more
I stood there all alone.

I left my castles in the sky
Wherein I dwelt awhile.
Back to the earth's reality
Each step it was a mile.

But then if I am patient
As sure as God's above
I'll find me castles once again
With those where I am loved.

M.A.F. Ketley

The Bee In the Hollyhocks

My hollyhocks have grown so tall
They overlook the garden wall,
They have no fragrance of their own
But flowers of red - and all full blown.

And you should see the honey bee
He comes and goes for all to see,
With yellowed legs like bags of gold
He carrys them like brigand bold.

He sips the dew right to its dregs
And having emptied both his legs,
Comes back for more – whilst er' the sun
Has only half its journey run.

You'd think he's free as up he flys
To reach the tallest near the skys
But lack alas! He cannot thrive
Without the sanction of the hive.

For drones are driven from their homes
No good are drones to honey – combs
That's why you see this busy bee
Working here so busily.

M.A.F. Ketley

The Missing Snowman

I wonder where our snowman's gone?
He's left his hat and pipe,
Do you think he's wandered off
Alone into the night?
Or did a band of pixies come
To take him to their queen
To dance and sing around him there
So strange to him, they'd seem!
Perhaps to us he will return
Adventures strange to tell,
Of elves and "fairy rings" in woods
Of gnomes and wishing wells.
But if he never comes again
To stand upon our lawn
When snow falls gently from the sky
We'll all feel so forlorn.
We'll have to make another one
With pipe and hat and all,
And watch him every minute
From daylight until fall.
Then perhaps we'll solve the mystery
Where snowmen vanish to,,
When children in their beds at night
Leave snowmen in the snow.

M.A.F. Ketley

The Nearness of You

To hold your hand and see you smile
To sit and talk with you a while,
These are the things that I long for
To see you near – I ask no more.
To hear your voice, and listen to
The everyday things that you do,
Your work, your leisure, hopes and fears.
The happiness, the joy, and tears.

Just one touch of your dear hand
Calls my soul to your command.
Tell me what you'd have me do
I'd move all Heaven and earth for you.
Seek no further for a love
Faithful ever – would I prove,
For no other shall erase
From my memory your dear face.

Swift as love's arrows should they come
I would bid them journey on,
For to me – you're all supreme
Waking or in sleep's deep dream.
For the sweetness of your love
I would gladly soar above,
Fly to where your heart maybe
Bring it back to bide with me.

And I would hold it ever dear
Close to my own heart sincere,
Heaven itself would not deny
This treasured love to you and I

M.A.F. Ketley

The Ploughing Match

I wander back along the lane- of golden memory
And in a field which fallow lies, a group of men I see.
The one who stands with head held high,
And hair as black as jet.
Has set himself a task this day,
To win an honest bet.

'Tis said for him who takes his plough and
horses as a team.
And draws the straightest furrows there
A handsome kettle wins.
'Tis copper bold, and shining bright,
Its belly full and round
'Twill later overflow tonight
Within the "Hare and Hounds".

Full half a dozen men set out
To bring them home the prize.
But only one left furrows straight
Now open to the skies.
His eyes are brown and shine beneath
His brow now damp and wet,
And with his kerchief wipes away
The beads of honest sweat.

They meet that night in local inn, And with their glasses high,
They toast the man that beat them fair
With straight and steady eye.
They know him for a Godly man
Who fears not friend or foe,
And proudly shakes him by the hand
As from the inn they go.

M.A.F. Ketley
To my Granddad Stimpson

To Heather with all my Love

If you should choose to read this book
When you are feeling low,
Take not my grief too seriously-
For surely you should know.

My moods are such that I one day,
Am way up in the clouds,
And then again I tend to fall
And wrap my heart in shrouds.

But like the sun that hides from view
Behind the darkest hour,
I always smile again – and so will you.
Hearts blossom sweeter – for a shower.

Mum

The Wonder Of You

You are the tallest tree
That stands within the forest deep
The brightest star, the moon that shines
While lonely eagles sleep,
The ceaseless wind-
That roams the mountains in its flight,
The oceans wide, the burning sands,
The seas by night.

The lovely daffodils, the clover sweet,
The country lane,
The fields of golden wheat,
The mossy banks, where robin's nests are found,
The rosy dawn,
The sweet earth, rich and brown.

I shall not want for sight of thee
Whilst all you are can come to me
In mountain peaks-
Now snowy white,
Or skeins of wild geese in their flight,
I seek thee in all worlds apart,
And lo! I find thee in my heart.

M.A.F. Ketley

To A Friend

When your heart has reached its lowest ebb
And skies are cold and grey,
When friends you had no longer care
And slowly drift away,
It is then you feel the need for prayer,
The need to search within –
To ask yourself the reason why?
And try again to win –
The love and sweet devotion
You know was once your own,
To hold it with a greater care
Than in the past you've shown.

And if you've done your level best
To show your love's sincere,
You'll find the happiness you seek
with love and more to spare.
It isn't what you have that counts
But more of what you are,
That lifts a man from depths unknown
To reach a shining star.

M.A.F. Ketley

To My Sweetheart

I'm writing a letter to you dear,
It comes right from my heart,
I wonder if you have ever thought dear
How far we are apart.
It seems I've lived a lifetime
Since first you went away,
I'm praying hard that you'll come back
To me dear again some day.

I treasure each of your letters dear
They prove a love that's true,
So today I am writing this letter
Saying I still love you too.
At night I lay awake thinking
Of times that seem so long ago,
When you and I have had scheming
A dream home just built for two.

I'm hoping with all my heart dear
Soon you'll come back to me,
From far away over the ocean
I'm praying for a calm sea.
So my darling please hurry home quickly
As soon as you possibly can,
I'll be waiting here for you always,
Yours forever your own sweetheart Nan

M.A.F. Ketley
Written at 12 years of age

To Jeanie On Her Flight to America

We thought of you my dear, as through
The hours we watched the face of time.
We raised our eyes, and sought the tumbling
Clouds – with you in mind.
Like mountain peaks they rose in splendour fair,
The setting sun beguiled all in view,
The cows were grazing still and quietly here
We thought of those last hours we spent with you.

When – glasses filled we toasted you – our friend,
And spoke of times we'd shared just you and we,
And though each bore a smile at memory's trend
Beneath there trembled tears for all to see.
And though a few more years may pass my dear
Before the sight of you will please our eyes,
I know our hearts will travel with you there
To be near you – beneath those torrid skies.

Let each and every day that you awake
Bring peace of mind, and happiness of heart.
And we shall keep in touch for old times sake
And never feel so very far apart.
Your letters are a treat we all enjoy
So keep them coming Jeanie good and fast
For we would share with you your future joy
As well as treasured memories from the past.

We see you here in everything we do.
We see you there in everything you tell.
We laugh again at jokes we shared with you,
And find we've shed a tear or two as well.
But these my dear, do not from sadness fall
But joy to know your cup is filled complete.
The past can only happiness recall
The future brings you everything that's sweet.

As sunshine warms the fragrance from the rose,
So does the thought of you beguile our days,
And you shall know that in our hearts there glows
Our love for you in Oh! So many ways.
So till we meet – we leave you in God's care,
His Blessing stay with you from day to day,
And hand in hand He'll walk beside you dear
To guide your footsteps all along the way.

M.A.F. Ketley

Written for our friend Jean and baby boy who were on the plane headed
for America to be with her husband in 1961.

To One Who Doubts

Have I not said I love thee
And need thy loving heart?
To keep mine own sweet company-
While we must stay apart

Have I not said I trust thee
With all this heart of mine?
Knowing quite sincerely
Your own with mine entwines

Have I not said I need thee
In every waking hour?,
Need the very warmth of thee
Like sun upon a flower

Oh yes! My dear – I love thee
And trust thee with mine all,
And need thee as no other can
With body heart and soul!

M.A.F. Ketley

Farewell To Love

The snow falls cold upon my heart today,
Small particles of ice they form
And turn my heart to clay,
Sad are my thoughts as they take icy wings
To cross the frozen fields –
No more to sing.

Farewell my love-
Sleep well across the years,
And should you think of me –
Think not with tears,
Better still, recall the golden hours we knew,
When happy in our love –
Our hearts were true.

The snow falls lighter now as if to say
"I'll cover not your dreams –
in one short day"
Be still my heart, and in a little while
You'll learn to sing again –
Perchance to smile.

M.A.F. Ketley

Fenland Fog

White world how still and quiet thou art
Outside my window pane,
As if no life exists out there
Or ever will again.
No wind, no birds, or fluttering leaf disturbs
This silent tomb,
Is this a world of fantasy?
And am I all alone?

M.A.F. Ketley

My Heart's Desire

If only I could write like Burns,
Byron, Shelly, or Rupert Brooks.
Perhaps my heart would cease to yearn
And outward could begin to look.

Though Autumn's cloth of gold is set
Beyond my window pane,
The winds are cold and grasses wet
And I withdraw again.

Withdraw into this shell of mine
A love where none can hope to meet,
To hold my hand in friendship fine
Or make my loneliness more sweet.

How can they understand my heart
When they have lost the key,
Have lost the warmth which was a part –
A part of life – and me.

M.A.F. Ketley

(Untitled)

Pink clusters of cherry and almond
As sweet as the blush of a rose,
Transform all the streets
And the gardens so neat
And away with the daffies that blows.

M.A.F. Ketley

By High Road and Low To "Home"

How I love the busy roads
On a Sunday afternoon,
Cars and people rushing past
As I bike out of town.
Some towards the seaside
In bright and sunny weather,
Some to take a picnic
'Mid woods and purple heather.

I love them all – their cheery grins
Makes travel worth the while;
Friends and strangers passing by
All ready with a smile.
I envy not their limousines
As I go on my way
To drink the sweetness of the air
Perfumed by new mown hay.

Each blade has known the falling rain
Each stem the morning sun-
Born into fields of buttercups
Kissed golden one by one.
I leave the busy highroad
And taker a quieter turn,
Past orchards plum and apple
Their spicy promise warm.

And clearly in the distance
My village church I see.
Reminding me of days gone by
And country fare for tea.
And somewhere in a cottage
Is someone I adore.
She's quite the dearest Mum on earth
And who would ask for more?

M. A. F. Ketley

CPSIA information can be obtained
at www.ICGtesting.com
Printed in the USA
BVOW10*0950240616

453089BV00004B/1/P